W9-APN-157

THE CREATION OF THE

Fantastic Four®

ERIC FEIN

The Rosen Publishing Group, Inc.,
New York

To my family—real-life superheroes

Published in 2007 by The Rosen Publishing Group, Inc.
29 East 21st Street, New York, NY 10010

First Edition

Thanks to Marvel Entertainment, Inc.: Avi Arad, James Hinton, Mary Law, Bruno Maglione, Tim Rothwell, Mickey Stern, Alberta Stewart, and Carl Suecoff

Library of Congress Cataloging-in-Publication Data

Fein, Eric.
The creation of the Fantastic Four/by Eric Fein.—1st ed.
    p. cm—(Action Heroes)
Includes bibliographical references and index.
ISBN 1-4042-0765-1 (library binding)
1. Fantastic Four (Fictitious characters) I. Title. II. Series.

PN6728.F33F45 2007
791.4'573—dc22

2005031170

Manufactured in the United States of America
On the Cover: The members of the Fantastic Four are the Human Torch, the Invisible Girl, the Thing and Mr. Fantastic *(from left)*.

CONTENTS

The Thing, the Invisible Woman, and Mr. Fantastic (*from left*) ascend into the sky while the Human Torch uses his firepower to fly in this page drawn by Alan Davis in 1998.

Reed, Sue, Johnny, and Ben are unlike any other Super Heroes of their time. The members of the Fantastic Four, a team of four superpowered people, did not set out to be superheroes. They gained their powers after being accidentally exposed to cosmic rays during a spaceflight. They also fight among each other. They are far from perfect, but they are good people at heart.

Reed Richards, the group's leader, is one of the smartest scientists in the world. He is called Mr. Fantastic because the cosmic rays gave him the ability to stretch his body like a rubber band. Mr. Fantastic feels responsible for exposing his friends to the cosmic rays.

Reed's wife, Susan Storm Richards, is called the Invisible Girl (later, her name was changed to the Invisible Woman) because she can make herself disappear. She can also create invisible force fields to protect herself and others. Her younger brother, Johnny Storm, is also a team member. He can generate flames that cover his body without burning himself. This is why he is called the Human Torch. His fire-power also allows him to fly.

The fourth member of the group is Benjamin Jacob Grimm, who is Reed's best friend and was his college roommate. The cosmic rays gave Ben superstrength, but at a price. The rays changed Ben's body in a horrible way. His skin became thick, hard, and orange. He looks like a walking pile of rocks, and his monsterlike appearance led to his alias, the Thing.

When Stan Lee and Jack Kirby created *The Fantastic Four* in 1961, the book was an instant success. *The Fantastic Four # 1* embodied a new direction for superhero comics—and little did the writer and the artist know in 1961 that their creation would soon influence all other superhero comics.

1 MEET STAN AND JACK

Stan Lee and Jack Kirby are comic book legends, but they did not start out that way at all. Both men came from very humble beginnings in New York City.

Jack Kirby was born Jacob Kurtzberg on August 28, 1917, to Benjamin and Rosemary Kurtzberg. Jack's father worked in the clothing business as a tailor. Jack's mother worked as a seamstress and sometimes in a bakery. Jack grew up in a very tough neighborhood on the Lower East Side of Manhattan. He learned very early how to fight, and throughout his life he never backed down from a bully. Jack always looked out for his younger brother, David, who was often teased by bullies.

Stan Lee is the older of two sons. He was born Stanley Martin Lieber on December 28, 1922, in New York City. His parents, Jack and Celia Lieber, were

Mr. Fantastic is Marvel's first character to have stretching powers. The most famous Super Hero with stretching powers is Plastic Man, who was created twenty years before Mr. Fantastic.

This is a 1972 photograph of Jack Kirby *(left)* with Joe Sinnott. It is estimated that Kirby drew more than 22,000 comic book pages. Of that number, about 2,200 pages were done for *The Fantastic Four.*

immigrants from Romania. The Lieber family was very poor; Stan's father worked as a dress cutter. During much of Stan's youth, the United States was enduring the Great Depression (1929–1939), a time when work was hard to get for most everybody. Stan saw his father struggle every day to find a way to make money. This affected Stan greatly, motivating him to work hard all his life.

A LOVE OF READING

Both Stan and Jack found relief from their hard lives by reading and going to the movies. From a very early age, Stan loved to read. He enjoyed books by a wide range of writers, including Edgar Rice Burroughs, Mark Twain, and William Shakespeare. Stan also loved to write. He even won some writing contests of a local newspaper.

As a child, Jack Kirby discovered pulp magazines. He loved their covers because they had fantastic images of aliens, spaceships, and monsters. He also liked newspaper comic strips: Hal Foster's *Prince*

Valiant was one of his favorites, and he also liked Milton Caniff's adventure comic strips. Jack taught himself how to draw by studying the works of Foster, Caniff, and other artists. By the age of nineteen, Jack was good enough to get work drawing newspaper editorials and comic strips. He also did work for the famous Max Fleischer animation studio. There, he drew pictures used for cartoons. After the Fleischer job, Jack worked for a company that produced comic book stories for a variety of publishers.

THE COMIC BOOK WORLD

Up until the mid-1930s, most comic books contained reprints of humor strips from newspapers. This is how they came to be called comic books. Super Hero comic books began in 1938, when DC Comics published *Action Comics* # 1, which introduced the world to Superman. *Action Comics* was an instant hit. Other comic book and pulp publishers saw this and wanted to get in on the money that could be made with Super Hero comic books.

One of the publishers to jump on the Super Hero trend was Martin Goodman. Goodman's publishing company got its start doing pulp magazines such as *Star Detective* and *Uncanny Stories*. Goodman was a big follower of trends. For example, when he saw a certain type of pulp was selling well, he would rush out his own version. It came as no surprise that when he saw how well Super Hero comics were selling he started his own line. The first comic book his company put out was *Marvel Comics* # 1 (1939). This issue featured two characters, the Human Torch and Prince Namor the Sub-Mariner, who would play important roles in the development of *The Fantastic Four*. Goodman called his comic book company Timely Comics. Over the years, Timely took on many different names. About 1963, it was officially named Marvel Comics, the same name it has today.

KIRBY'S RISE

In 1939, Kirby had moved on to Fox Features Syndicate, which also produced comic book stories. It was here that Kirby met Joe Simon, a writer and artist. While Simon was working for Fox, he was also creating projects for other companies on the side. Kirby, wanting to earn more money, asked Simon if he needed help. Simon agreed, and soon the newly formed team was turning out many comic book stories.

In early 1940, Goodman hired Simon to be the editor of Marvel's comic book line. Simon, in turn, hired Kirby to help him co-create comic books for Marvel. The two also worked with freelance writers, pencillers, inkers, colorists, and letterers. Simon and Kirby co-created many different characters, but unfortunately, few, if any, caught on with comic book readers. That all changed when Simon and Kirby co-created Captain America. He was a superpowered soldier designed to fight Adolf Hitler and the Nazis. *Captain America Comics* # 1 went on sale in December 1940. It was a huge hit, selling a million copies.

This was great for Simon and Kirby, who found themselves even busier than before. They needed help around the office, so they asked Goodman for an office assistant.

LEE'S RISE

Stan Lee heard about the office assistant job up at Goodman's comic book company through a family connection. Goodman was married to Lee's cousin, and while Lee and Goodman were in-laws, they had hardly met before Lee got the job. At the age of seventeen, Stan Lee began his comic book career, and his duties included such tasks as running errands, handling the mail, and proofreading. It was as an office helper that Stan Lee first met his future professional partner, the artist Jack Kirby. In *The Jack Kirby Collector*, Kirby talks about the early days of his and Lee's acquaintanceship, which gave no hints about their fateful collaboration in the future: "He [Lee] was a young fellow, and we were just nodding acquaintances … We got along … There was no evidence that we'd ever get together in any way as editor and artist."

Lee was a determined young man who was eager to become a professional writer. He got his big break when Simon and Kirby gave him an assignment to write a two-page text story, "Captain America Foils the Traitor's Revenge," for *Captain America* # 3. Two issues later, in *Captain America* # 5, Lee's first true comic book story, "Headline Hunter, Foreign Correspondent," was printed. Shortly after Lee started at Marvel, Simon and Kirby quit because of

Stan Lee continues to create new characters and concepts for use in comic books, movies, and television. As a child he loved reading William Shakespeare. The influence of the Bard's rhythmic and flowery language can be found in Lee's scripting of characters such as the Silver Surfer, Thor, and Dr. Strange.

a falling out they'd had with Martin Goodman over business. With that, Lee, the office aide and burgeoning writer, was made editor of the company's comic book line.

STAN AND JACK GO TO WAR

Both Lee and Kirby served in World War II (1939–1945). In the early 1940s, Lee was still the editor at Marvel Comics, and Kirby was still doing work for several comic book publishers with Joe Simon.

Lee was in the army from 1942 until 1945. During his enlistment, he wrote training films and manuals that were used to educate soldiers on using weapons and equipment and following army rules. Lee never saw combat, but he did see the country by working at different U.S. Army bases.

Kirby, who served in the army from 1943 until 1945, was sent overseas to fight in the war. The army made use of Kirby's skills, too. He was made a scout, or somebody whose mission is to find information about an enemy's plans. His job was to draw maps and pictures of anything that might have been of importance to the army. Kirby and a few other soldiers would advance ahead of their unit, entering towns to see if the enemy was present, and then he'd make his

WHAT'S IN A NAME?

Stan Lee and Jack Kirby, like many other authors and illustrators at the time, chose to use pen names. Back then, comic books were not viewed as a respectable industry in which to earn money. Lee never planned on making comics his life's work. He always wanted to write a "great American novel." So, he turned his first name, Stanley, into Stan Lee. Lee also used other pen names, including Stan Martin and Neel Nats.

Jack Kirby used different names because he drew stories for several different publishers at the same time. Using pen names and working for several publishers were standard practice back then. Two of Kirby's pen names were Jack Curtis and Jack Cortez.

sketches to give to his commanders. This was a very dangerous job. Many scouts, if captured, were beaten or killed.

BACK TO WORK

In 1945, with the end of the war, both Lee and Kirby returned to their former jobs. They found the comic book world had changed. Super Hero comics were no longer as popular as they once were, and comic book publishers were looking for new kinds of stories. Jack Kirby and Joe Simon went back to working together. They co-created the romance comic book—love stories told in comic book form. Their first title was *Young Romance*, which was published in 1947 and was very successful.

Other publishers soon started doing their own romance comic books. At Marvel Comics, Lee worked on Western comic books, war comic books, monster comic books, humor comic books, and romance comic books.

COMIC BOOKS ARE EVIL!

In the early to mid-1950s, comic books suffered a decline in popularity and sales. A belief that comic books caused children to misbehave and even commit crimes had begun to spread. The U.S. Congress even held hearings about the matter. The negative publicity hurt publishers, and many went out of business. Others, including Marvel, dramatically cut back on their output.

Around this time, Kirby and Simon went into business for themselves and started Mainline Comics. They produced titles such as *Bullseye, Western Scout,* and *Foxhole*. However, the company did not last long. Kirby and Simon had disagreements, and eventually, their venture fell victim to the times and personal conflicts. By the mid-1950s, their partnership was over.

At that time, Kirby went to work for DC Comics, but he soon found himself without any work from the company. Many on the DC Comics staff viewed him as an outsider. He then went back to Marvel and began drawing comic book stories featuring giant Godzilla-like monsters for such titles as *Journey into Mystery* and *Tales to Astonish*. Lee wrote these stories. This marked the first time that Lee and Kirby worked together as a creative team. This also marked the beginning of something special.

2 A WORLD OF CHANGE

When Lee and Kirby co-created the Fantastic Four in 1961, the country was going through big changes. America was in the middle of the Cold War with the Soviet Union, and the threat of a nuclear war hung over the world.

Meanwhile, the United States and the Soviet Union were also in a race to see who would control outer space. The Soviets had successfully launched several spacecrafts in the late 1950s. The National Aeronautics and Space Administration (NASA) ran the space program on the U.S. side, and the agency was determined to put a person on the moon. One of its first successes came in 1961, when astronaut Alan Shepard became the first American sent into space.

At home, the civil rights movement was getting stronger. People began protesting to demand equal rights for African Americans and other minorities. Young Americans began to question the policies of the U.S. government. The U.S. government was getting involved in the Vietnam War (1964–1975), which divided Americans.

These shifts in culture were reflected in movies, TV shows, and music that came out during the 1960s. While it seemed that popular culture reflected the turmoil of the times, comic books were slow to show the changes in American life.

DC COMICS SUPER HEROES

By the early 1960s, there were only a handful of comic book companies left, compared to the dozens and dozens of publishers in business in the 1940s. DC Comics was home to Super Heroes such as Superman and Batman. Back in 1956, DC Comics had begun redoing some of its older heroes, such as the Flash. The Flash was a Super Hero with the power of superspeed. Under the guidance of editor Julius "Julie" Schwartz, DC gave some of its characters new origins and a more modern look. The changes were very popular with comic book readers.

Around 1960, DC Comics teamed its newly popular heroes the Flash, Green Lantern, Aquaman, and the Martian Manhunter with its time-tested heroes Superman, Batman, and Wonder Woman. The series was called *Justice League of America*. It was a big seller for the company.

THE MARVEL AGE OF COMICS

As soon as Martin Goodman heard about how well *Justice League of America* was selling, he went to Lee. He told Lee to come up with a book just like it. He suggested Lee use some old Marvel characters such as Captain America, the Human Torch, and the Sub-Mariner. However, Lee had ideas of his own.

Up until that moment, Lee had been working mostly on the Godzilla-like monster comic books with artists such as Jack Kirby and Steve Ditko. (Ditko would go on to co-create *The Amazing Spider-Man* with Stan Lee in 1962.) Lee felt that Goodman did not respect his hard work and talent. After twenty years in the comic book business, doing work that he loved, he wanted to quit.

Lee's wife, Joan, knew that he was unhappy with his job, and when he told her about the new project, she encouraged him to put every ounce of his creativity into it. She wanted him finally to do comic books the way he thought they should be done. That way, if he was fired, he would have no regrets.

Lee had no interest in doing the Super Hero book that used existing characters. Instead, he wanted to start from scratch. Lee did make one concession to Goodman. He used the name and powers of the Human Torch. The original character was an android, or human-looking robot, that had flame powers. Lee wrote a plot synopsis, or story summary, for the book.

Lee assigned Jack Kirby to the book. The two spoke about the characters and the story. Kirby took Lee's story summary and went off to draw the book. The finished book was *The Fantastic Four # 1*, and at the time, neither Lee nor Kirby knew that their new co-creation would keep them busy for years to come.

A NEW BREED OF SUPER HEROES

The heroes of *The Fantastic Four # 1* were very different from the DC Comics Super Heroes. One of the major differences was that *The Fantastic Four* was a character-driven book. This means that Lee and Kirby were more interested in how the characters developed as people. Where they traveled and whom they fought were of lesser importance. Other comic book companies emphasized the plot more than the characters.

THE FANTASTIC TWO

Stan Lee and Jack Kirby worked together as seamlessly as their stories flowed. *Comics Creators on Fantastic Four* quotes Lee's statements about Jack Kirby's work and his admiration for him: "After we started *Fantastic Four*, I realized that he was absolutely unsurpassed as a visual storyteller. He was also great at coming up with ideas within the stories and also coming up with entire stories himself ... They [the characters] always had a defined expression on their faces and their body language always told the story."

The respect was mutual. In a 1969 interview with Shel Dorf and Rich Rubenfeld, printed in *The Jack Kirby Collector*, Kirby commented on his return to Marvel in the late 1950s and his work with Lee: "I went to work for Stan Lee, and whatever Stan Lee's policies are, they're my policies. Whatever kind of job Stan Lee wants done, I will do that job. I feel that is the artist's job; to cooperate with the policy of the publishing house. I've always done that."

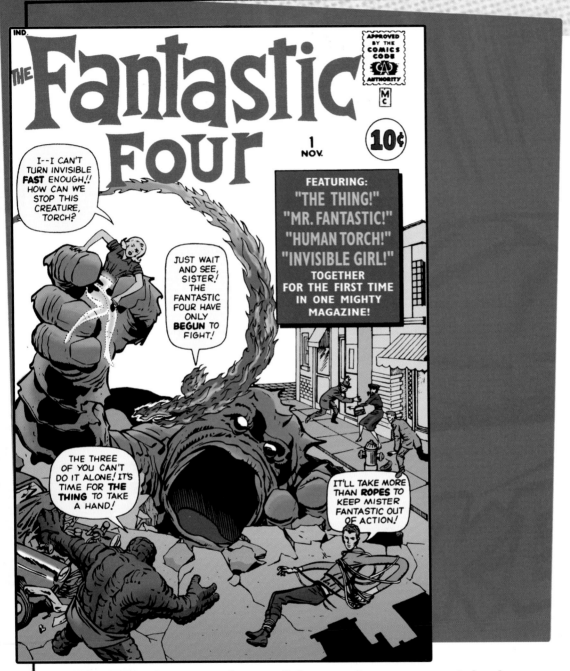

The *Fantastic Four* # 1 is one of the most important comic books ever produced. It set a standard that comic book professionals still try to match. Because the characters are not in costumes, the book appeared to be more of a monster comic book than an superhero comic book. Today, a copy of *The Fantastic Four* # 1 is valued at about $25,000, and the price continues to rise.

Lee and Kirby's heroes were different from the standard Super Heroes of the time, who had very simple motivations and flat character traits. The members of the Fantastic Four argued among themselves, and they had their own unique flaws. Ben Grimm, the Thing, looked like a monster and not like a hero. Johnny Storm, the Human Torch, was a hot-tempered teenager. In most Super Hero comics, the woman was a love interest who usually needed to be rescued by the hero. Sue Storm, the Invisible Woman, was, however, an equal member of the team. She was also the glue that held the Fantastic Four together and was usually the peacemaker between the other members of the team.

A SENSE OF CONTINUITY

Most comic book stories at the time had one or two self-contained stories. Usually, there were no discussions or references by any of the characters about what had happened in previous issues. Lee and Kirby crafted their stories so that they continued from one issue to the next. This gave the series a sense of progression. Over the next few years, as Lee and his artists co-created more Super Hero series, they tied all the comic books together. This created the effect of continuity, or one shared fictional universe. Things that happened in one series were mentioned in another.

About a year or so after the Human Torch's introduction in *The Fantastic Four*, he was given his own series in *Strange Tales*, running from issues 100 through 134.

THE WORLD'S GREATEST COMICS MAGAZINE

The look and feel of the Fantastic Four have changed over the years. This is especially true during Lee and Kirby's time on the book. It took Jack Kirby some time to get the look of the characters just right. The look of the Human Torch changed between his first appearances in *The Fantastic Four* # 1 to *The Fantastic Four* # 3. Originally, he looked more like a mass of flames with limbs. Over time, Kirby changed Johnny's appearance to become a more recognizable human form. It took a bit longer for Kirby to develop a look he was happy with for the Thing. The Thing started out looking like a lumpy, apelike creature. By the mid-1960s, he had a more angular look. The Thing looked more like a walking pile of rocks, which were actually protective plates. Kirby got the idea for the Thing's look after doing research on dinosaurs, many of which had armor-like plates that protected their bodies.

While he was always considered a master artist, his early work on *The Fantastic Four* had a very rough look to it. Part of the reason for this was that Kirby had many different inkers finishing his work. They were all very talented; however, Lee felt that none of them gave the book the look he wanted. That changed with *The Fantastic Four* # 44, when Joe Sinnott became the regular inker. Sinnott gave Kirby's art a slick, bold look. The fans liked this new look.

FRIENDS AND FAMILY

Lee and Kirby co-created a wonderful supporting cast for the Fantastic Four. They gave the Thing a girlfriend, Alicia Masters. She is a blind artist who carves statues. Though blind, she is able to "see" the good man trapped inside the Thing. Alicia is also the stepdaughter of one of the Fantastic Four's enemies, the Puppet Master. Reed and Sue have a son, Franklin. He is born in *The Fantastic Four Annual* # 6. This added a new aspect to the heroes' lives. Sue now has to deal with matters that most working mothers have to deal with. She takes time off from the team to raise her son.

The Inhumans are a race of superpowered beings. They start out as enemies of the Fantastic Four, but eventually, the two groups are able to work out their problems and become close friends. In fact, two Inhumans, Medusa and Crystal, take turns filling in for Sue when she leaves the group to raise Franklin.

This *The Fantastic Four* page shows Kirby and Sinnott at the height of their artistic powers. Sinnott was one of the most popular inkers ever to work at Marvel. In addition to *The Fantastic Four*, Sinnott inked many other Marvel series, including *Thor* and *Captain America*.

BRING ON THE BAD GUYS

Lee and Kirby understood that great heroes needed to battle great villains. They co-created dozens of memorable foes for the Fantastic Four. The Skrulls are shape-changing aliens determined to conquer Earth. Galactus and the Silver Surfer are threats from outer space. Galactus is a huge and powerful being. He is about 29 feet (8.9 meters) tall and weighs about 18 tons (16 metric tons). However, since he is so powerful, he can alter his size and shape. He travels the universe consuming the energy of different planets, destroying them in the process. The Silver Surfer is Galactus's herald, or official messenger. His job is to find new planets for Galactus to destroy. The story played out over three issues of *The Fantastic Four* (# 48–50) and has come to be known as the Galactus Trilogy. During the story, the Silver Surfer betrays Galactus and helps the Fantastic Four save Earth.

Lee and Kirby brought back Prince Namor the Sub-Mariner. Namor is the ruler of the undersea world of Atlantis. However, Lee and Kirby came up with a storyline that had Namor angry at the surface world for ruining Atlantis. It takes years, but Namor eventually makes peace with the Fantastic Four.

Dr. Victor Von Doom, considered one of the greatest comic book villains ever created, is the ruler of Latveria, a nation in the Marvel Universe. He is a brilliant scientist who is also trained in black

THE FIRST BLACK SUPER HERO

In *The Fantastic Four* # 52 and 53, Lee and Kirby introduced the first black Super Hero. Sadly, there had never been a hero of color in comic books up until that time (1966). Lee and Kirby named him the Black Panther. This was months before the black power group called the Black Panthers made itself known to the world.

The Black Panther's real name was T'Challa, and he was the king of an African nation called Wakanda in the Marvel Universe. Creating a black Super Hero was a bold move on the part of Lee and Kirby. At the time, the country was divided over issues of race. However, the Black Panther proved to be very popular. He soon turned up in many other Marvel comic books. Today, the Black Panther has his own ongoing series, *The Black Panther*.

Today, the Black Panther is the star of his own comic book series. It is written by Reginald Hudlin, who also wrote the *House Party* movies.

magic. He wears an armored faceplate after receiving injuries from an experiment that blew up in his face when he was at college. Reed Richards was one of his classmates at the time, and he had warned Doom that he had made a mistake in setting up his experiment. However, Doom ignored him. Over the years, Doom starts to blame Reed for the accident. In addition to his armored faceplate, he wears full body armor and a hooded cloak.

THE METHOD OF CREATION

Before Lee and Kirby started on a new issue of *The Fantastic Four*, they would talk about it. Kirby sometimes worked in the Marvel offices in New York City. Most of the time, he worked at home on Long Island, and he and Lee would talk the story out over the phone. They would decide who the villain would be and on the major action scenes. They would also decide what subplots, or secondary storylines, would get attention. Then Kirby would draw the story over twenty-two pages. He would add scenes and characters

When Lee and Kirby co-created the Silver Surfer in 1966, they hadn't thought up an origin for him. The character did not get an origin story until 1968, when Lee, working with artist John Buscema, launched the character in his own ongoing series, *The Silver Surfer*. This page shows Galactus confronting Norrin Radd, a citizen of the planet Zenn-La. Radd agrees to become Galactus's herald in order to spare his home world from destruction. A few pages later, Galactus turns him into the Silver Surfer.

This page from *The Fantastic Four* shows Dr. Doom after he has stolen the Silver Surfer's powers. The black dots coming from Doom's hands represent energy and are called Kirby Krackle, in honor of their creator.

when he thought it was necessary. This way of creating a comic book came to be known as the Marvel Method. Lee developed this process during his years as an editor and writer. Usually, artists would draw from a full script, or a panel-by-panel breakdown of the story. These scripts also contained the text for captions and dialogue. Writing full scripts takes a lot of time.

Lee explains the process in an interview in *The Jack Kirby Collector*: "In the beginning, I'd give him [Kirby] written-out plots … After a while I would just tell him what I thought the story ought to be. Then after a while, I would just give him a few words. He could practically do the whole thing by himself … Very often I didn't even know what … he was going to give me … I turned it into whatever story I wanted it to be."

THE FANTASTIC FOUR AFTER STAN AND JACK

By 1970, Jack Kirby was ready for a change. He wanted more creative control over his work, and he left Marvel and went back to DC Comics. There, he had a deal to write, edit, and draw his own comic books. As the 1960s were coming to an end, Stan Lee had been taking on more work on the business side of Marvel. He began to give up many of the regular books he was writing. He stepped away from writing *The Fantastic Four* a few months after Kirby left. Together, Lee and Kirby produced 102 issues of *The Fantastic Four* as well as six forty-eight-page annuals. They accomplished all of this from 1961 to 1970. It is an achievement that few writer-and-artist teams have ever matched.

Over the years, other talented writers and artists have worked on *The Fantastic Four*. Series writers have included Roy Thomas, Marv Wolfman, Gerry Conway, and Mark Waid. Artists who have worked on the series are John Buscema, Paul Ryan, George Perez, and Mike McKone.

In the 1980s, John Byrne took over the book during a time when it was not as popular as it had once been. He both wrote and drew *The Fantastic Four* and is credited with bringing back a sense of awe and adventure to the book. He also changed Sue Richards's name from the Invisible Girl to the Invisible Woman.

The Thing is one of the most popular characters in the Marvel Universe. Not unlike Kirby himself, the Thing grew up in a tough neighborhood. Kirby and Lee also gave the Thing the battle cry, "It's clobberin' time!"

4 MAKE MINE MARVEL

The Fantastic Four # 1 struck a nerve with comic book readers. Lee quickly realized this when hundreds of letters began flooding Marvel's offices. Readers felt strongly about the characters; each had his or her own favorites. The fan letters contained smart observations about the characters, stories, and art.

EXCELSIOR!

Lee was fun-loving and outgoing. He loved being around people. This came out in his writing and approach to comic books. Lee was also not afraid to break the dramatic mood of the stories. He would use captions and footnotes to speak as the writer directly to the reader. Sometimes he would write a funny comment about the unbelievable situation the heroes were in. Other times, such as in footnotes, he would point out other Marvel comic books for the readers to buy. Lee also wrote the letters pages and the Bullpen Bulletins. He used the letters pages as a way to have a conversation with the readers. Sometimes, readers would find mistakes in the art or story. Instead of ignoring it or getting upset, Lee published the letters they sent telling him about his mistakes. He gave these readers an award called a No-Prize. It was just an empty envelope sent to the readers, and they loved it!

The Bullpen Bulletins let readers know what was happening at the Marvel offices. The bullpen was an actual area at Marvel where some artists and production people worked. The bulletins were printed in every Marvel comic book, and they let the fans know what was on sale that week and what was coming up. He also told stories about all the fun that was being had by the Marvel staff at the office. He signed each bulletin with the phrase "Excelsior!" "Excelsior" is an expression that means "ever upward." This became his catchphrase, and he still uses it today.

FOR THE TEENAGE FANS

The Fantastic Four became quite popular very quickly. Originally, it was published every other month. That was soon changed to every month. Lee was so confident in the book's success that he added a disputable declaration on the cover of every issue, starting with # 3. The motto, in its most typical form, proclaimed that *The Fantastic*

Four was "The World's Greatest Comics Magazine!" Lee did this in part to tease the other comic book publishers. He also did it as a joke. The joke, however, turned out to have some truth to it.

Martin Goodman, seeing a great opportunity to make more money, urged Lee to co-create more Super Hero comic books. Lee did not let him—or his readers—down.

Because of his success, Lee now could do comic books the way he thought they should be done. Even though most comic book readers were children or teenagers, he never simplified for them. He did not shy away from using big words. The worst that could happen, he figured, would be that a child would have to look up a word in the dictionary.

The Fantastic Four and the other Marvel comic books that followed it became very popular on college campuses. Some colleges

"THIS MAN, THIS MONSTER"

"This Man, This Monster" is considered one of the greatest Fantastic Four stories of all time. Comic book readers, comic book historians, and comic book professionals (writers, pencillers, inkers, editors, etc.) agree for the most part on this point. Published in *The Fantastic Four* # 51, the story covers many of the themes and ideas found in modern comic books: heroism, friendship, responsibility, and what it means to sacrifice one life for another. It also looks at what happens when someone feels like an outsider in society. The plot focuses on a mad scientist who steals the Thing's power and appearance. The scientist does this so he can destroy the Fantastic Four. But after he sees how much the team members care for each other, he changes his mind. During the course of the story, he gives his life to save Reed's.

began to offer courses on the Marvel Super Heroes as a study of modern mythology or folktales. Student organizations invited Lee to give lectures, and he did.

Lee, as editor and writer, was very aware of the impact his books were having on teenagers. He also understood that the mood of the country was changing. This, in turn, affected the way teenagers looked at the world. Lee and Kirby were very good at co-creating characters that tapped into the emotions of their readers. During the 1960s, many teens began to question authority, and authority figures included their parents, teachers, and the government. Super Heroes that represented authority, such as Superman, were becoming less popular.

Lee and Kirby gave teenagers heroes with whom they could identify. Reed, Sue, Johnny, and Ben all struggled to find peace in their lives. They wrestled with many of the same questions that teenagers did: Who am I? Where is my place in society? Teenagers especially identified with Johnny Storm. He was the youngest member, and adults did not always take him seriously. Also, like most teenagers, Johnny questioned authority. It did not matter to him that Reed was the leader. If Johnny didn't agree with Reed, he would often disobey his orders. This was something that was unheard of in comic books at the time—for instance, Robin never argued with Batman.

5 FANTASTIC TODAY AND TOMORROW

The popularity of the Fantastic Four has had its high and low periods over the years. However, the influence of the series has never lessened. At Marvel, the success of *The Fantastic Four* motivated the company to co-create other teams of Super Heroes. Marvel introduced *The Avengers* and *The X-Men* in 1963. Both were written by Lee and drawn by Kirby. These series featured characters that did not always get along and had doubts about their place in the world.

DC COMICS RESPONDS

When Marvel's sales began to climb, DC Comics did nothing. Many there thought Marvel was just a fad. This way of thinking was gone by the late 1960s. DC Comics could

Dr. Doom is considered one of the greatest villains in comic book history. His influence can be seen in Darth Vader from the *Star Wars* movies.

no longer ignore Marvel's success. DC Comics began to inject more reality into its books. However, it could not duplicate the Marvel style across its own line of books. It took years for the gap between the two companies to narrow. In the 1980s, DC Comics introduced *The New Teen Titans*, a series about a band of young characters that included established characters such as Robin, Kid Flash, and Wonder Girl. It also included new characters such as Cyborg, Raven, and Starfire. The book was written and drawn by two Marvel—and *The Fantastic Four*—veterans: Marv Wolfman and George Perez. They blended space adventures with extremely character-driven stories. In an interview in *Back Issue* # 7, Marv Wolfman said, "Everyone always said my Teen Titans was DC's X-Men. Couldn't be further from the truth, since I was never an X-Men fan. I always said my Titans was DC's FF."

THE FANTASTIC FOUR AND HOLLYWOOD

Early on, Hollywood took notice of the Fantastic Four. The team was the star of no fewer than three different animated TV series. For years Marvel had tried to get a Fantastic Four movie made. After many false starts, the Fantastic Four finally reached the big screen on July 8, 2005. Produced and released by 20th Century Fox, the movie received mixed reviews from film critics. The filmmakers altered the origins of the Fantastic Four and Dr. Doom. In the movie, Doom is not the ruler of Latveria. He is a rich businessman, like Donald Trump. Also, Doom took part in the spaceflight that gave the team its powers. In the movie, the cosmic rays' effect on Doom is that he

In an effort to bring in new readers, Marvel reenergized and updated the Fantastic Four with its *Ultimate Fantastic Four* series. Marvel's Ultimate books used dynamic visuals to bring in the cinematic energy of recent Marvel hit movies. The panel above by artist Adam Kubert is from *Ultimate Fantastic Four #5*. It features the Thing, (top panel, center), Mr. Fantastic (top panel, center blue figure), and the Human Torch (top panel, right) fighting one of the Mole Man's giant monsters.

slowly turns metallic. Some comic book fans were unhappy with the changes the filmmakers made.

Despite the mixed reviews from critics and upset comic book fans, moviegoers loved the movie. *Fantastic Four* did capture the sense of fun and the family relationships between the characters. It made $100 million in its first two weeks, guaranteeing that the team would return in a sequel.

STAN AND JACK AFTER *THE FANTASTIC FOUR*

Lee and Kirby continued to have successful careers after they left *The Fantastic Four*. Both moved to California, although at separate times and to different places. Kirby continued to do comic book work as well as work on animated shows for kids. He returned briefly to Marvel in the mid-1970s, when he wrote and penciled *Captain America*. He also co-created new series, including *Machine Man*, *Devil*

THE FANTASTIC INCREDIBLES

The Fantastic Four as a team of Super Heroes has been an inspiration in other areas of popular culture. The premise of a family of Super Heroes can be found in the Disney/Pixar movie *The Incredibles*. Many comic book fans and comic book professionals noted the similarities between the Incredibles and the Fantastic Four. For one, the word "incredible" echoes "fantastic." Mr. Incredible is super-strong like the Thing. His wife, Elastigirl, has stretching powers like Mr. Fantastic. Their daughter, Violet, can turn invisible and generate force fields. Both powers are just like that of the Invisible Woman. Their son Dash has the power of superspeed. Though his power does not match any of the Fantastic Four's, his personality does. Dash has the Human Torch's playful and at times troublemaking nature. Finally, baby Jack-Jack has the same ability as the Human Torch to create flames at will. The movie was a huge hit in theaters and on DVD.

Dash, Violet, Mr. Incredible, and Elastigirl *(from left)* are the Incredibles.

Dinosaur, and *The Eternals*. He worked on several projects for DC Comics in the 1980s.

Lee continued to do occasional writing work for Marvel. In 2000, he did a series of comic books for DC Comics featuring his versions of such characters as Batman and Superman. Today, Lee runs POW Entertainment, a company that develops new characters for movies, television, and the Internet.

Today, *The Fantastic Four* remains an important series for Marvel Comics. The series has been around for nearly forty-five years and close to 540 issues. Over the years, Reed, Sue, Johnny, and Ben have also played important roles in other Marvel titles. They have guest-starred in *The X-Men* and *The Amazing Spider-Man*. Reed and Sue even became members of the Avengers for a short period of time. The Fantastic Four has also been featured in many limited series and one-shot, special-edition comic books. From 1974 to 1983, Marvel published *Marvel Two-in-One*. This comic book series starred the Thing. In each issue, he teams up with a different Marvel Super Hero. It lasted for 100 issues. When that series ended, Ben Grimm was given his own ongoing solo series, aptly titled *The Thing*. It was published for 36 issues, from 1983 to 1986.

Currently, the Fantastic Four star in several ongoing series: *The Fantastic Four, Ultimate Fantastic Four, Marvel Knights 4,* and *Marvel Adventures: Fantastic Four*. A new ongoing series featuring the Thing debuted in late 2005. The team is also still featured in many one-shot specials, limited series, and reprint collections.

After Lee moved to California, he shifted his focus toward Hollywood, trying to persuade movie studios to make movies and TV shows out of Marvel characters. Kirby, after five decades of working on comics he loved, took on less and less work as he got older and became ill. After a battle with cancer, he died of a heart attack on February 6, 1994.

The series that two New Yorkers co-created has survived wars and major political and cultural changes in the United States, and it has acted as the springboard for a new type of heroes possessing superpowers and human flaws. The project that Jack Kirby and Stan Lee began more than four decades ago still thrives and lives on. For Marvel, its readers, and Reed, Sue, Ben, and Johnny, the future is guaranteed to be … fantastic!

STAN LEE AND JACK KIRBY TIMELINE

1917 Jack Kirby is born on August 28 in New York City.

1922 Stan Lee is born on December 28 in New York City.

1940 Lee goes to work at Martin Goodman's Timely Comics (later known as Marvel Comics). Kirby (as well as his partner, Joe Simon) stops working for Marvel Comics. Lee becomes the editor and main writer at Marvel.

1958 Kirby returns to Marvel Comics and begins working with Lee.

1961 Lee and Kirby co-create *The Fantastic Four* and launch what has come to be known as the Marvel Age of Comics.

1962 Lee and Kirby co-create *The Incredible Hulk*. Lee, along with artist Steve Ditko, co-creates *The Amazing Spider-Man*.

1970 Jack Kirby leaves Marvel to go to work for DC Comics.

1978 Lee and Kirby work together one last time. They co-create a Silver Surfer graphic novel.

1985 Kirby does the last major comic book of his career, *Hunger Dogs*, for DC Comics. It featured New Gods characters he co-created for the company back in 1970.

1994 Jack Kirby dies.

2000 Lee writes a series of comic books for DC Comics. These books feature Lee's versions of Superman, Batman, Wonder Woman, and other heroes.

2002 Lee starts a new company, POW Entertainment.

2005 *The Fantastic Four* (the movie) is released.

THE FANTASTIC FOUR HIGHLIGHTS

1961 *The Fantastic Four # 1:* Reed, Sue, Johnny, and Ben gain their super-powers during a flight into space. They fight their first Super Villain, the Mole Man.

1962 *The Fantastic Four # 3:* The Fantastic Four wear Super Hero costumes for the first time.

The Fantastic Four # 4: They fight Prince Namor the Sub-Mariner.

The Fantastic Four # 5: Dr. Doom makes his first appearance.

The Fantastic Four # 8: The Puppet Master and his stepdaughter, Alicia Masters, are introduced.

1963 *The Fantastic Four # 12:* The Fantastic Four have their first meeting with the Incredible Hulk.

1965 *The Fantastic Four Annual # 3:* Reed and Sue get married.

The Fantastic Four # 45: The Inhumans first appear as a group.

1966 *The Fantastic Four # 48:* Part 1 of the Galactus Trilogy. This issue introduces the Silver Surfer and Galactus.

The Fantastic Four # 50: The Galactus Trilogy ends. Johnny goes to college.

The Fantastic Four # 52: The Black Panther makes his first appearance.

1968 *The Fantastic Four Annual # 6:* Reed and Sue's son, Franklin Richards, is born.

1970 *The Fantastic Four # 102:* This is the last issue of *The Fantastic Four* that Lee and Kirby do together.

41

GLOSSARY

colorists The artists who use colored inks, dyes, and markers to create color guides for the printers. Colorists color copies of the inked art. Today, most coloring is done with computers.

continuity The consistency within a story or stories, as in, for example, the entire Marvel Universe. Continuity in that context deals with the relationships between hundreds of characters, and events.

inker The artist who uses black ink to complete a penciller's artwork, readying it for reproduction.

origin The story of how a superhero came to be.

penciller The artist who tells the story in visual form, determining the page and panel composition that best allows the reader to follow the story.

pulp magazine Cheap fiction magazines, usually dedicated to a subject such as science fiction. Named "pulps" for the newsprint on which they were published (the cheapest kind of paper available for printing), they usually had attention-getting covers. These magazines originated prior to paperback books and were hugely successful between the 1920s and 1950s.

script Similar to a movie script, a comic-book script breaks a story down into individual pages, describing the action for each panel.

FOR MORE INFORMATION

Museum of Comic and Cartoon Art
594 Broadway, Suite 401
New York, NY 10012
(212) 254-3511
Web site: http://www.moccany.org

WEB SITES

Due to the changing nature of Internet links, the Rosen Publishing Group, Inc., has developed an online list of Web sites related to the subject of this book. This site is updated regularly. Please use this link to access the list:

http://www.rosenlinks.com/crah/four

You can also refer to Marvel's Web site:

http://www.marvel.com

FOR FURTHER READING

Byrne, John. *Fantastic Four Visionaries: John Byrne.*
Vol. 1–4. New York, NY: Marvel Comics, 2001.

Kirby, Jack, Joe Simon, and Stan Lee. *Marvel Visionaries: Jack Kirby.* New York, NY: Marvel Comics, 2004.

Lee, Stan, and Jack Kirby. *Essential Fantastic Four.*
Vol. 1–4. New York, NY: Marvel Comics, 2005.

Lee, Stan, Jack Kirby, John Romita, and Steve Ditko.
Marvel Visionaries: Stan Lee. New York, NY: Marvel Comics, 2005.

Thomas, Roy, and George Perez. *Fantastic Four Visionaries: George Perez.* Vol. 1. New York, NY: Marvel Comics, 2005.

BIBLIOGRAPHY

Bailey, Blake. *The 60s*. New York, NY: Mallard Press, 1992.

Cooke, Jon B. "Stan Lee Interview." *The Jack Kirby Collector*, Vol. 9, No. 33, 2006, pp. 58–62.

Daniels, Les. *Marvel: Five Fabulous Decades of the World's Greatest Comics*. New York, NY: Harry N. Abrams, 1991.

DeFalco, Tom. *Comics Creators on Fantastic Four*. London, England: Titan Books, 2005.

DeFalco, Tom. *Fantastic Four: The Ultimate Guide*. New York, NY: DK Publishing, 2005.

Dorf, Shel, and Rich Rubenfeld. "Innerview." *The Jack Kirby Collector*, Vol. 10, No. 37, 2003, pp. 50–53.

Greenberger, Robert. *Will Eisner*. New York, NY: Rosen Publishing Group, 2005.

Jones, Gerard, and Will Jacobs. *The Comic Book Heroes*. New York, NY: Crown Publishers, 1985.

Lee, Stan, and George Mair. *Excelsior! The Amazing Life of Stan Lee*. New York, NY: Fireside, 2002.

Lee, Stan, and Jack Kirby. *The Fantastic Four Omnibus*. Vol. 1. New York, NY: Marvel Comics, 2005.

Mallory, Michael. *Marvel: The Characters and Their Universe*. New York, NY: Hugh Lauter Levin Associates, 2001.

Overstreet, Robert. *The Overstreet Comic Book Price Guide.* 31st ed. Timonium, MD: Gemstone Publishing, 2001.

Raphel, Jordan, and Tom Spurgeon. *Stan Lee and the Rise and Fall of the American Comic Book.* Chicago, IL: Chicago Review Press, 2003.

Ro, Ronin. *Tales to Astonish.* New York, NY: Bloomsbury, 2004.

Wright, Bradford W. *Comic Book Nation.* Baltimore, MD: Johns Hopkins University Press, 2001.

INDEX

ABOUT THE AUTHOR

Eric Fein has worked for both Marvel and DC Comics. At Marvel he edited several Spider-Man comic book series, including *Spider-Man*, *Spectacular Spider-Man*, and *Web of Spider-Man*. He also co-edited the first team-up of Spider-Man and Batman. At DC Comics he edited storybooks, coloring and activity books, and how-to-draw books featuring DC Comics Super Heroes such as Superman, Batman, and Wonder Woman. Currently, he is developing and writing several different book and comic book projects.

CREDITS

p. 8 courtesy of Mark Sinnott; p. 12 © Kim Kulish/Corbis; p. 37 © Walt Disney Pictures/Pixar Animation/Bureau L.A. Collection/Corbis. All other images provided by Marvel Entertainment, Inc.

Designer: Thomas Forget
Editor: Jun Lim
Photo Researcher: Les Kanturek